ALSO BY ANNETTE HOLLANDER

Scenes from My Trip: Poems, 1998-2010

How To Help- Your Child Have a Spiritual Life:
A Parent's Guide to Inner Development

WHAT YOU ALWAYS WANTED TO KNOW

Poems 2010-2020

ANNETTE HOLLANDER

FCP

Full Court Press
Englewood Cliffs, New Jersey

Published in the United States of America
by Full Court Press, 601 Palisade Avenue,
Englewood Cliffs, NJ 07632
fullcourtpress.com

ISBN 978-1-946989-87-1
Library of Congress Control No. 2020925259x

Editing and book design by Barry Sheinkopf

Cover photograph by the author

"When Does It Stop?–A Haibun" originally appeared in
Contemporary Haibun Online (CHO).

"Hosting" will appear in an anthology entitled *Corona.*

ACKNOWLEDGEMENTS

I would like to thank the Madison Poets: Ana Doina, Mary Himmelweit, Maria Lisella, Arlene Metrick, Jimmy Roberts, Ann Settel, and Jeffrey Steinberg, for years of inspiration, nourishment, and editing. Thanks also to my friends Lisa Commager, Jane Goldsmith, and Michael Laikin for needed editing, and to my husband, Myron Kaplan, with whom I have shared poems for fifty years.

WHAT IS A HAIBUN?

Haibun (not a well-known term) is a poetry form, originally Japanese, that combines a prose poem with a haiku.

"There is general agreement about what haibun is attempting: a marriage between prose and haiku in which the two are equal partners. As in good marriages, the partners grow through their intimacy; by combining their individual talents they are stronger as a duality than either partner would be on his or her own."

—David Cobb

TABLE OF CONTENTS

WHAT YOU ALWAYS WANTED TO KNOW
(Homage to Epicurus)

What you always wanted to know
is what I wish I could tell you:
What happened?
Why?
What exactly is happening now,
and what can you do about it?
Will it matter that you lived?
And to whom?

One of the mightiest questions, of course,
is about the Big Bang—
who or what lit the fuse, and why?
Some astronomers say it will happen again,
after our universe contracts. Maybe that will be
one more chance to find out.

All-knowing would foresee trouble—
then no reason to get out of bed—
but this ignorance is like poverty,
and we all are desperately poor.
If you are a believer,
your God knows all the answers
and even dictated some of them
but still left many questions
for sages to debate.

Sorry, I fooled you. I don't have any answers.
I only have the questions—
but let us sit a while and enjoy them
over a glass of good wine.

A CAN OF MANY WORMS
(For Ana Doina)

otherwise known as a family
after the parents die,
wrestling without referees;
no one to blow the whistle
on a flagrant foul.

Siblings once loving
want to grab what they can
short of getting lawyers involved—
because lawyers take all—
but without lawyers or parents
who's to say what's fair?
Mom and Dad taught fairness,
but that was then.
The grown children
make up their own minds.

There are no rules now.
What I want/what you want
what they would have wanted
could be shuffled like cards
or spun around in a bingo cage,
but randomness isn't fair either.

All feel put-upon.
Who takes advantage of whom?
Who's to say?
Envy the Englishmen
their rules of primogeniture,
although history tells us
some got poisoned.

Sometimes, by chance
it all ends up even,
and everybody's happy.
This happens when there's nothing to divide,
or when there's only one child.

If only people could be satisfied with what they get—
But then we wouldn't be human, would we?

A Year In Haiku/Senryu

Winter

Night falls at teatime
I'd like to sleep until spring
Settle for three naps

Spring

Snow crocus pushes
Through winter's mulch
Opens its blue eyes

Summer

A dark summer night
The rain writes down
Many poems

Camping on Mount Hood
I can still feel the tree root
Under my sleeping bag

After Falling in Poison Ivy

Tossing in my bed
Like a fish out of water
I yearn for the lake

Fall

People drive away
The summer house says goodbye
Oaks wave sorrowfully

ABSTRACT BUT SO TRUE

I know
Nothing about some things,
Something about many things,
A lot about nothing.

I wish I knew more.

My busy brain
Whirs tirelessly,
Making connections
Cross-referencing,
Forgetting.

AGE

I don't want to talk about it
I want to be what you see in front of you
no transparent stage curtain
revealing clumsy stagehands

If I don't pay any mind to it
perhaps the edifice will stand
unperturbed by rotten wood
under the eaves

Cracks in plaster are subtle
until the plaster falls
Little mistakes can be meaningless
or not

What you see depends on
what you're looking for
I don't want to give you clues
so I don't want to talk about it

All My Landmarks Have Changed

so I don't know where I am going
or where I've been.
Wasn't the path to the meadow
just around the bend?
Who moved the rock?
That oak looks different in the moonlight.

It used to be so easy.
I just had to look for the mailbox—
but the grass has grown high,
and anyway, that was long ago.

I could always let someone else navigate,
but that admits failure
to know the land like my own body,
the swellings and hollows.
Why not stay here?

Almost The Solstice—Summer

Slow sunset time
Allowing myself to be here

A lone butterfly cloud
floats through blue air

Say hello to my friend Lynn
who lives across the water

Every third blade of beach grass
is covered in gold leaf

So much hurrying to get stuff done
Not now

Grateful for all of it

Almost The Solstice—Winter

(December 12, 2019)

It is not winter yet, but I can see
piles of leaves, bare branches, and the sky
color of no imagination. I
know the sun isn't low as it will be
in nine days, but today was pretty bad—
the taxi got lost, I had to stiff my friend
to drive my husband into town. In the end,
though, nobody died. Earlier I was sad,
but now I'm laughing. That's the way things turn—
up and down, like the flighty sun and the seasons.
We'd better get used to it, stop looking for reasons,
expect to freeze and then expect to burn.
At the solstice for a moment the sun stands still,
but as long as we're alive, we never will.

AMBIVALENT ODE TO MY SKIN

You may kill me someday,
but I am grateful for the way
you keep me alive for now,
protecting me from life forms
that want to make my body their home.

All my organs deserve thanks,
but you are the one I see the most,
and you give me so much pleasure
when touched the right way.
We won't mention pain.

Although fascia, not skin,
holds me together,
you present me to the world.
Years ago, smooth glowing skin
radiated beauty,
but what you show now is damage
from years at the beach.
Inside I don't feel damaged,
but nobody sees inside.

Some spots are just potholes.
Others may be cells gone rogue
that want to grow forever,
even if they kill me—
which brings me back
to the beginning of this ode
where I celebrate you—
provisionally.

APRIL BIRTHDAY

Trees celebrate,
Waving their newly green leaves–
It is my birthday

Each birthday
Finishes a race–
Then time for another

Seventy-eighth year–
The first time
I worry about age

Bushes bright yellow,
Trees pink and white bloom today
For my birthday

APRIL NAP HAIKU

Spring breeze on my cheek
yesterday we put up screens
sleep is in the air

AT MY AGE

The light runs away (won't wait)
as I set out on the trail to catch it,
above my head now
but I can climb faster
to where gold glazes
the middle of trees.
Finally—my shadow!
I have arrived—
briefly—
and then have to hurry
to snatch a photo
of the stream, shining,
which I do, but then
darkening (no more shining)
and I have to turn
downhill
to the horizon,
able, now,
to look the final sun
directly in the eye.

AUTUMN EQUINOX

Today
when day and night are balanced,
so am I,
standing on one foot
arms outstretched
one side basking in the sun
the other catching falling leaves.

How tempting to demonize the coming dark
as I slide toward icy skin, feel black moods.
But I could be sad in the sunshine
glow on a snowy night.
We are not plants, predetermined
to live underground until spring.
Snatch this moment, peel it,
Press its juice,
taste and drink.

"BE ASSURED, YOU ARE NOT ALONE."

> "Toward evening, the natural light becomes intelligent
> and answers, without demur, 'Be assured! You are not
> alone. . .'"
> —*from* "Descartes' Loneliness," *by Allen Grossman*

We need to hear that everywhere—
songs, the Bible, posters on the subway
We can't hear it often enough
from morning light to sunset
because it can be lonely inside this skin-bag
So please, talk into my voice recorder
and say in a soothing deep voice
"Be assured, you are not alone"
Tell me again and again
(there is truth in repetition)
And one day, your voice
will keep me company as I walk
around my house
and through the universe
and that will be all
I need

BEING ALIVE

It is fascinating being me
and you
and that bush on the terrace—
we share the same stuff:
molecules of beginnings and ends
genes that push and pull
surroundings that nourish or kill

Some poets feel kinship with mountains
Not this one
Sun and moon are good company-
with me every day-
but not part of my family
the way you are
and that bush

People complain about family
but without family we are lonely
People complain more about being alone
Death holds no terror
when boundaries dissolve
As now, in the elevator
I stand next to a newborn part
of this family
who does what newborns do:
She looks at me, then starts to cry.

Being Old

Being old
is to be irrelevant
to the busy-ness of the world,
to the kids on the street
in their odd clothes
whistling unknown tunes.
Pop Culture
belongs to the Martians.
Celebrities are strangers.
Fortunately the radio
plays Oldies
while I tend my garden,
one foot in the mud,
dodging mosquitoes,
contemplating dahlias.

CHANGE OF STATE

Ice becomes water,
which disappears into air.

The word liminal
means "threshold".
Can we know when we are liminal,
not on one side or another?

Molecules of water
can't be half water, half ice
but a puddle can.

My mindbody
is a puddle
only half old.
I'd like to stay here
on the threshold.

CHERRY BLOSSOMS DON'T CARE—A HAIBUN

Cherry blossoms don't care
about coronavirus carried on the breeze.
Bright yellow daffodils
poke up through the ground as usual.
Signs of spring keep pace with the pandemic, growing,
exploding:
grass and magnolias, yesterday a dandelion.
Today Jenny took sick.
Spring sunshine, filled with illness.
This season needs a new name:
Summer, fall, winter, fear. . . .

    Red-breasted robin
    Pulling worms out of the ground
    Right on schedule

Chutzpah—A Haibun

When life brings you lemons, use chutzpah:
Some examples:

1932. Depression in America, poverty. My Jewish
mother teaches dance to nuns, although she cannot
dance. She takes a lesson, then teaches it.

1969. The Women's Movement is just beginning to
growl in America, and I need a job. I say to the head of
the medical Fellowship, "I think you need a woman in
your program," and he makes me a Fellow.

2016: My daughter, tired of working with warring
couples, wants to teach, finds a course for first-year
graduate students that interests her. The dean says:
"I see you're not exactly qualified, but nobody else
applied." He gives her a faculty position.

> Dogs raise their hackles
> To look bigger than they are,
> Win without fighting.

Cleaning The Basement: Lessons From The Buddha

Why did I cling to this stuff—
     leather holster for a letter opener long gone,
     toddler's sorting blocks without the box to sort them,
     toilet paper printed like ticker tape?

Hard to get rid of stuff unless it's repurposed:
Obsolete fax machines
will donate their organs;
I do hope those speakers with the booming bass
(which take too much power)
find a good home,
and boxes of unworn sneakers find happy feet.

We can see the floor of the room now
after we carted off:
     the model horse collection
     old videotapes
     a massage table.
Little ones will play here again
with games their mothers played,
some of which still have their pieces.

Such attachment to stuff
creates disorder—
let go, if you can.
It is a life's work
like weeding, knowing the weeds will come back,
although that's no reason not to try—
it's like saying why bother living
since we know we are going to die?
So with a joyful heart

and a peaceful mind
I'm hauling my stuff
to the thrift store
and the recycling dump.

Then I will buy birthday presents
for my children's children.

COME TO YOUR SENSES

You work so hard
to increase the length
of your days.
Make them *wider*.
You remember what you see and do—
all interesting, of course—
but sight and motion
are only the beginning. . . .

Go into your day
leading with your nose.
Except for perfume or stench,
scent is usually ignored,
but like wine-lovers,
you may find hints
of berries and chocolate.
Savor the taste of your soup.

Do days have texture?
Linen and silk,
or studded with nails?
And sounds—
let them come
through the mind's filter:
traffic and birdsong.

So many sensations wait for you
in every moment.

Comeuppance By Coronavirus

I could never force millions of people
all over the world to have *my* children!
Little creature with no brain
wins the replication contest.
This virus doesn't *do* anything
except create copies
and make people sick.
What a waste of life force
(from my point of view.)
Here we are, proud *homo sapiens*
at the summit of the ladder of creation,
about to be toppled from the bottom.

CREATION MYTH

Our people tell the story of how long ago
when there was nothing, not even stars, or gods,
Maestra created herself in this way:
First stardust, that became her long black hair,
then the sun, so she could see her creation unfold,
then earth, for a body when needed,
then water to make rain and oceans.
Coyote came and said:
We need something to make us laugh,
so they created people
and plants and animals to feed them.

And all lived happily for many years
until one of the snakes said:
Why should I be only one of many snakes.
I want to be Lord of the Snakes.
So he drove out all the other snakes,
who had to find new homes.
When the people and the other animals saw this,
they said: *Why can't we be Lords, too?*
So they fought until only one of each was Lord.

When Maestra saw this, she was not pleased,
so she sent a flood.
Coyote said: *Let's try again.*
Perhaps we can do better this time.
Then, as our ancestors tell,
the gods came down to talk to people,
explaining that if they wanted to continue to live,
they had to follow these rules:

"Before you act, imagine that
You are the one receiving your action."

"We will do that," said the people.

And for many generations all was well,
until one man asked, *"Who here has talked to a god?"*
and no one spoke.
"You see, the gods left us long ago.
Now we can make our own rules."

Maestra and Coyote were not pleased
with the stupidity of their own creation.
But this time they did not even bother
to send a flood.
They just left.

CROSSWORD PUZZLE OF NEW YORK, FOR A NEW YORKER
(for Jimmy Roberts)

Streets with patched potholes
Cross splendid avenues
Anyone can play
Clues to moments of our lives
Fill the intersecting squares
And you can write it

CULL BAMBI!

I see stillborn lilies,
roses that never had a chance,
deer bellies full of my darlings.
A fawn crawled under my fence—
and they are not even starving.
Spring rains brought green everywhere,
but deer pass up grass and weeds
for my tulips
so that, well nourished,
they can have triplets
instead of twins.
Our forest, too, suffers:
understory eaten leaf and branch,
no more baby trees,
no future generation when parents fall.
Sometime soon,
this ravenous herd, ballooning,
will die of starvation
after consuming all their resources,
just like us.

CURTAINS

Do people ever say, "Curtains," any more
to mean the end of something, the final act?
I always loved Broadway theater,
watching heavy velvet drapes,
waiting for the show to start.
The curtain would rise, or part with tantalizing slow-
ness,
and no matter what, people would applaud.

We want our lives to make a story
with beginning, middle, and end.
Suffering people can get "narrative therapy" (really!)
or take a memoir-writing class,
turn bad times into drama.

A mystery writer explained his secret:
"Start with a question," he said.
"We are programmed to keep reading
until we find the answer. That's called 'suspense'."

Every baby is a question
racing to find an answer
in a life full of suspense,
before the curtain drops.

DARK UNIVERSE

(After the "Dark Universe" Space Show at the Hayden
Planetarium)

Unseeable even by scientists,
dark energy and dark matter now
fill most of our universe,
where our little visible piece—
all we have to view
walk in or under
(even stars)—
used to be enough

Who needs fairies, ghosts, goblins?
Science has taken us past the limits
of imagination

Deconstructing A Self—A Haibun

I spent years putting it together; now I am taking it apart
one vanity at a time.
As I discover how disposable it is
(I can always find what I need)
I travel lighter,
Smile more.

When I am mad at myself
With whom, exactly, am I angry, and who is angry?

Gaze into dark pond
Is that a smile or a frown
Broken by ripples?

Deconstructing Joy

I live for moments of joy:
Flute music, sunset, poems about sunset;
your touch.
Sandalwood burning in yoga class.
Chocolate in any form will do it,
also grandkids,
and that purple crocus
peeking out of last year's leaves.

Between that crocus and my joy
we need chemicals, electricity–
as sensory nerves to the brain
run signals from synapse to final synapse
in a tiny brain region
which lights us up with *Joy*
But first I have to pay attention.

Developmental Milestones of My Grandchildren

Eli, 14, takes off his shirt every day at the beach,
gets tan front and back, unafraid of sunburn,
flaunts his "six-pack" and muscular shoulders.

Sister Becky, 12, makes me cry
when I ask her to help me.
She looks me in the eye and says, "No."
Another milestone?

Leah, 12, wants another week in tennis camp
(she's not very good at tennis)
because Ryan is there.

Isaac, 9, just traveled alone on a two-hour bus ride,
but still sleeps in his parents' bedroom when he can.
Does that count?

What's next? I bite my nails—
even though I passed these milestones long ago
on my way to here.

DIALOGUE WITH DONALD
(Donald Horwitz, 1933–2020)

Me: Hello, Donald. Lola says that you died May 31.

Donald: Yes, Lola would say that.

Me: Well, what would *you* say?

D: Since you saw my body only four or five times in the last half
century, this really isn't so different for you, is it?

Me: A little.

D: You see?

A: Now that you're here, I have a couple of confessions.

D: Tell me.

A: I always wanted to be your editor. You had so many interesting
things to say, in essays or poems, but you did it in your very odd
style. I wanted to make you more "accessible."

D: God gave me the gift of speech. Who am I to question God?"

D. Tell everybody why you introduced me to Lola. I was always cu-
rious what you were thinking.

A: I don't remember exactly. I know you were both living in New
York and single (I was in Cambridge, still in college), so that
was a good start. And that's what friends are for.

D: Yes, but why Lola?

A: Well, you were both smart and interesting, but the right person
for you would also have to share your love of classical music.
Lola, a pianist and beautiful, seemed a logical choice.

D: I thank you for this.

A: Lola has thanked me too, though I have wondered over the
years how she could thank me; you could be so stubborn. But
don't get me wrong. Now I understand: If you love a genius,
you love someone who is unique in every way, including annoy-
ing ones. Do we know what Einstein's wife thought about his
hair?

D: No, we don't. But what makes you think you can herd me into a
poem and expect me to stay there? If people want to hear my
words, let them read my books.

A: I'm sorry, Donald. But Lola wanted anecdotes, and I couldn't remember any. I feel really bad about it.

D: That's all right, sweetie. You know I love you just as you are.

A: Thank you, Donald. That's just what I wanted to say about you.

DIANA FESTA
(*July 9, 1930--June 8, 2011*)

You and I met as elders with an even older teacher
The other poets could have been our children

In your salon, you gathered us together to make word-
music
You sang of love and loss

Petite Earth-Mother,
You made heaps of food emerge from your tiny kitchen

You rolled the raw dough of our poems
Spiced them; knew when they were done

You could see the bones of a good poem
Inside the blubber

Adjectives: gracious, warm, welcoming, modest
Wise, precise, delicate, firm
How can I choose without you here to help me?

At the end, you were ready to go
I am not ready to let you be gone

DOUBLE ELEGIES

1. Two Stars of the Women's Movement

> "We are coming down from our pedestal and up from the laundry."
> —*Bella Abzug, 1920–1998*
>
> "It is easier to live through someone else than to become complete yourself."
> —*Betty Friedan, 1921–2006*

I didn't know either of you
but I know what you did for women—
you made waves

You weren't pretty –
Okay, let's face it, you were homely –
but you got things done

And I always wondered
how it would feel
not to have to please people—
just be a force to be reckoned with.
Until people did what was right.

I'm glad you didn't live
to see women's rights retreat
without a Bella to face down the bullies,
or Betty to start a revolution

I just hope your life's work
was not in vain
and that I keep you in mind
the next time I want to appease.

2. Two Men Who Entertained Us

"Reality is just a crutch for people who can't cope with drugs."
— *Robin Williams, 1951–2014*

"How therapeutic it is to surround yourself with people stranger than yourself."
— *Spalding Grey—1941-2004*

I still can't figure it out, Robin,
how you could be funny while miserable
I mean *very* funny while *very* miserable

You tried to kill yourself with booze, cocaine
and I can't figure out
how your family kept loving you

And you were able to make the whole world love you
when you couldn't love yourself
I just can't figure it out.

Spalding, how could you go onstage,
entertain an audience,
and then go home and try to jump off a bridge?

And even stranger, this happened over and over.
Your family knew, but what could they do?
Lock you in a cave?

You were famous— a celebrity
but no fame could stop you
from drowning in the East River,
or you, Robin, from hanging yourself.

(No one realized that Williams died suffering from Lewy body dementia.)

DYSTOPIA

What's a dystopia?
It's what we have, only more of it:
fire and flood and war destroying homes;
leaders making themselves rich while people starve;
land nothing will grow in, and air no one can breathe.
All these things are happening,
so we don't need imagination.
Through the ages—
plenty of dystopias, no utopias.
The world I want, it seems,
has never existed.
Unfair–if you can have one extreme,
Why not the other?

I know why we can never have utopia:
In a world where everyone cooperates,
all secure and happy,
any aggressor
can quickly dominate,
grab all the resources,
make *themselves* happy.
No one is ready for this;
no one fights back.
They try to be reasonable,
in utopia.
My wish: for one of our genes to mutate,
make us *all* less selfish,
reverse direction,
roll toward utopia.

Each Summer

Part fish, part mermaid,
I glide through water,
swim through rays of sunlight,
now and then balancing on my ear to breathe.

When summer ends
I cannot bear my exile
from that liquid land
where I have no weight and no thoughts.

I must get back
before my joints stiffen
and I think it normal
to put one heavy foot in front of the other.

Release me from this bucket—
let me slide into the welcoming sea,
back to the womb,
and before. . . .

ELECTION 2016: TO BE READ ALOUD

I.
The ache in my belly tells me that someone has died,
but no one has. Only a dream has died.
"You're an idealist," my husband says
sneering a little. I used to be proud of it.
Now ideals hang like an albatross around my neck:
the dream that men would treat women as equals,
the dream that we would respect each other,
appreciate how people come in different colors;
the dream that humans could reverse the damage to our planet.

I grieve because half the people in my nation
chose a leader who despises my dreams.
He's bad, but worse is that the spiral staircase of progress
has no more steps, in my future at least;
we will be forced to turn around, walk back down,
and one out of every two people I meet
want it like that.
They are no longer my brothers and sisters.
And inhabitants of my nation are no longer family,
not the enemy, certainly–just alien beings.

I grieve the belief good things will happen in my lifetime.
I grieve for the world my children will live in.
What made it worse was the suddenness:
unexpected bomb appearing over the horizon
while I slept, awakening to rubble.

How can I not be melodramatic when my heart is broken?
Forgive me, I was unprepared.

2.
I feel like the husband
of a woman who just died in childbirth
going home, having to pass the nursery,
freshly painted.

I feel like I was in the hospital
having been run over,
except it was the nation
run over by its own people.

I feel like a tightrope walker
who slips,
blaming herself for being so sure
she could do it;
I would like to pull in all my tentacles
like an octopus, hide
in a hole in the rocks.
Then I could forget what happened:
how my neighbors chose as leader
a woman-hating dictator
bent on undoing my life's work.
I know this happens;
history could have taught me.
But I would have said,
"Not here, not now."

Today I feel foolish
A toddler who refuses to understand the word
"No."

ELECTIVE CANCER SURGERY

"Wyrd oft nereth unfaegne eorl, thonne his ellen deah."
(Fate often spares the man of undaunted courage, if
destiny allows.)

—*Beowulf*

From intact to broken
voluntarily——
is that madness?
Just because machines say
danger lurks inside?
No animal would choose this:
pain on purpose
where there was none,
possible impotence
and definite leakage
replacing passion
just because a number is high
and cells look ugly under a microscope.

This is the curse of being human:
knowing the future—sort of—
knowing we will die—though not exactly when—
compiling statistics.
Statistics say I will live longer cut up,
so I invite the knife,
that like Beowulf's "Unfaegne eorl"
I may avoid my fate
if destiny allows.

ELEGY FOR SALLY PEREZ
(June 13, 1962 – July 4, 2015)

Sally,
You did what you had to do.
For one, you got back at those bitches your sisters
who wanted to evict you in two months
from the home where you had nursed their mother.
And George, that SOB,
will be sorry
for saying he never loved you,
and wanted to leave you––
some thanks for the years you took care
of his obese, diabetic, bedridden self,
jumping to his every whim.
But now, even if he changed his mind,
you were too weak to clean his diapers,
and you couldn't see living alone
with constant pain and nausea
without him.
He was your reason for living,
(none of your friends understood why)
and now you were convinced
he wanted you out of his life.

> *I thought you should go to a hospital*
> *when you kept getting weaker––*
> *from vomiting and malnutrition,*
> *not just depression,*
> *felt confused from pain medicine,*
> *too unsteady to drive.*
> *But you refused to go to a hospital*
> *even when the paramedics said you were having*
> *a heart attack.*

You did me a favor
by not calling me that last week.
If you had told me you wanted to kill yourself
I would have had to hospitalize you.
I would have had to take away
all you had left, your self-respect.
I knew you wanted to drop dead—
but you reassured me, lying, "Catholics don't suicide."

You were proud of having survived
a life of endless abuse
That started in childhood, both parents.
When you had a good job,
you got fired for refusing to have sex with the boss.
You took care of everyone except yourself,
even giving the wicked sisters presents
when you had no money.
Now there was no one who wanted your care.

What we were doing those last months
wasn't therapy,
since you always refused
to act in your own self-interest.
All I could give was what you wanted—
sympathy-
and occasionally suggestions you resisted.
But then even sympathy didn't help——
your situation was so dire.
I knew it.
You knew it.
I only wish we had been able to say goodbye.

So goodbye, Sally.
May you find in death
the peace that eluded you in life
and may tonight's July 4th fireworks
attended by thousands
be the memorial service
a selfless person like you deserves.

Estate Planning

I can't bequeath my life to my kids—
everyone has to live her own.

Which of my stuff is a burden,
and what smells of good memories?
Money to buy new stuff
is always welcome,
as are words of love,
but sibling rivalry
clings to each page of my will.
Love will not erase it
any more than a kiss cures an infection.

We do what we can
to nurture our children
all our lives
and after.

ESTRANGEMENT

> "The two most important days in your life are the day you
> were born and the day you find out why."
> —*Mark Twain*

What happened to you when you turned thirteen?
You said, "Nobody knows me,"
which I believe
because you shut us out a year ago.
It wasn't pleasant for me either.
I watched, helpless, as you drifted away on your ice floe.
You felt desperate, approaching thirteen,
couldn't see the future at all,
didn't want to stay alive.
I wrote you a poem describing you as a "pupa"
struggling to emerge from your pupa case,
wanting to show you I understood.
You admitted you felt stuck "half in and half out,"
but you didn't want to hear about
how I too had been depressed at thirteen.
Since I'd lived to tell the tale,
I thought my wisdom could help you,
but you weren't having any.
All I could do was visit you in the hospital.

I so wanted to be the grandmother I never had,
who could help you feel not guilty
for wriggling out when Mommy clutched too tight
or a grandfather who could teach you
the thirteen logical fallacies
(the way my father taught me at thirteen)
so that no politician could ever fool you.

You once asked me, "What is the purpose of life?"

so I wrote a poem begging you, beloved girl,
to stay alive long enough to find yours.
I fear you may not let me back in before that,
though now you are laughing and smiling again.

You and I had always bonded over words—
reading the same novels—
but now you only read Stephen King,
and I don't like to be scared.

Eulogy For Anne Barry
(1941–2013)

She's still sitting there, laughing
waiting for death
keeping busy while waiting
like someone knitting in a doctor's office.

She's still making us laugh
about anything and everything
like a good sit-down comic
while we try not to stare at her oxygen machine.

Send me an e-mail, Anne,
from the other side,
so that I'll know you're really gone,
stop waiting for the next post.

You mastered the art
of talking about your troubles without complaining.
You received needed care and attention
in return for which you offered wisdom

that all of us will need someday,
because all of us will die,
but we don't like to think about it,
which brings me back to not wanting to say "Goodbye."

Goodbye, Anne.
Thank you for a well-lived life. . .and death
(which was never easy)
and for letting us see how that is done.

EULOGY FOR ANNE DAVIS
(Read to Anne before she died)

You are slipping away from me
like houses out the rearview window.

It is hard to feel from your point of view—
that maybe you are done with pain and helplessness—
because I selfishly want to keep you with me,
but you will be the fish that got away.

Someone suggested telling you how dear you have been:
how cheerful in the face of years in a wheelchair,
rounds of chemotherapy,
all that time giving us attention and empathy
as well as good food.
Yes, I would like you to know,
but it makes me want to hold on.

Wait a minute, who needs comfort here?
Anne with the radiant smile?
Probably, but also all who love her.

I can count on you not to make *me* suffer,
and that is why losing you will be such a loss.

EULOGY FOR S.M.

You died yesterday by your own hand.
unwilling to live in constant pain,
unable to walk to the corner store.
Were you brave or a coward?

Smiling, teasing, making us laugh—
your vitality, like the sun
made *us* (your friends, all the family you had)
feel alive—
but the sun is supposed to live
for a few more million years.
Feeble people expire—not you—
and certainly not willingly.

We all need models of courage,
which you were:
going to Chile with a shaman,
starting the first humanistic medical clinic in the U.S.,
first cancer support group in Brazil.

Your body's defection stopped all that.
You wrote, *I, who have always believed that we can do it!*
That I can do it! And patterned my life somewhat
after a favorite childhood tale of "The Little Engine That Could,"
just can't.

You dreaded an end
as a burden to others,
or having doctors make your decisions.
You wanted to die the way you lived,
by "doing it,"
and did.

EVEN YOUR COMPUTER

"Even your computer is a haunted ruin."
—*Robert Pinsky*

Cities wait for the earthquake
Basements for the flood
Even your computer will be a haunted ruin

But now your computer is a gift
To make you godlike, all-seeing
Vessel for the wisdom of the world

Except when your computer makes you feel stupid
Crashing around you
While everyone else thrives

Poor pretty machine
Faithfully crunching its numbers
Infected with our metaphors
Our feelings

FALSE PROMISES

Little green nails of daffodil tips
poke through dead leaves today.
I want to hammer them back down
before their enthusiasm is broken
by the next arctic vortex.

That man on the ski slope today
was wearing shorts—
people so eager to jail-break from winter
they ignore the storm troopers waiting.

Nevertheless,
I too shed coat and hat and gloves like everyone else.
Last year's fake spring
left us with frozen peach blossoms,
no peaches in August.

Dark-hearted,
I hold on to my gloom about the world.
Today is like last election day, with its broken promises.
I won't
be fooled into a smile,
even if everyone around seems cheerful.

Innocents! Don't they know
they will soon be shivering under blankets
while ice murders those daffodils?

Family Choreography

In the dance of who's right, who's wrong—
endless—
you won't give up,
and I don't want to.
Is this a necessary dance, such as
between reality and illusion,
sun and moon?
Is it lethal
like cat and mouse?

I long to watch the dance of yin and yang—
of all that is—
without freeze-framing it:
today, your angry lips
smiled a few minutes later
at Maia in her tutu
and patent leather shoes
prancing on a wooden floor,
while little brother, waiting outside,
wriggled to his own music.

FERRIS WHEEL

Hooting,
my family dangles
on top of the Ferris wheel.

I am on the ground,
clenching my teeth.

Why do people like to be scared
when life is terrifying?
I watch my daughters
make their little seat
swing into the air
high above carnival grounds.
They are laughing.

The wheel jerks to its next level.
A couple on the bottom lift their bar
and step on solid ground.
That couple just lived the old joke:
"Stop the world—I want to get off!"
In life, that's suicidal.
The rest of us hold on with white knuckles
and enjoy the view.

First-World Problems

I can't complain to my kids
about having to vacuum and do laundry
because we are in quarantine
and the cleaning lady can't come.
"First-world problems" they sneer,
And they are so right.
My Tibetan pen pal, suffering from TB,
must sweep the monastery every day
without complaining.
I wish I knew more about the texture of her life
aside from her prayers.
In novels I swept the dirt floor of my hut,
with the heroine, carried out ashes, and hauled in water.
In *my* house, two days without internet was stifling.
I shove my husband over when he hogs our king-sized bed.
In other lands, husband, wife, and children share the bed
but, when given their own beds, crawl in together anyway.
I'm not talking about lacking food, clothing, or shelter—
a disaster for anyone.
I say we dislike what we're not used to—
first, second, or third world.

FLIGHT FEATHERS
(*for Rascal*)

You took flight
in the most shocking way,
little bird who did not sing but said, *"Hello!"*
We never knew to call you "he" or "she,"
So we used both.

Rainy and cold today—good funeral weather.
Live birds everywhere:
ducks in the pond, lovebirds in our daughter's house,
swans on the Sound,
while Rascal's cage sits empty
except for old newspaper.

How to explain it to the kids?
Say the spirit that made him move
has left this limp body,
still green as the rain forest,
still capped with peach,
But where did it go?
Nobody knows.
(Unsatisfactory answer.)
And why?
Because he got old.
(Unsatisfactory answer.)

You were a good pet.
You will be missed.
Goodbye.
"Hello."

For Janet

You were fierce
and you were determined
but even that
couldn't make
Death wait outside the door.

For Stanley (1905–2006)

"I am not done with my changes"
— Stanley Kunitz, *"The Layers"*

My father quoted:
The only thing that stays the same is change.
He was 63 at the time.
I was 13 and thought that was hogwash.

Stanley, writing at 100, knew what he was talking about.
He had no fear of his next change
because he was a gardener,
understood and loved
the changes in his garden:
the necessity of winter,
the necessity of death.

Forest Age Six

Little boy shot from a cannon,
breaking rocks with a hammer and chisel,
chasing your sister around my living room,
I'm so glad I'm your Nana, not your mother.

Patient like a true fisherman
even when the fish aren't biting–
why is it *only*
when fishing?

Swim like a shark, climb like a tiger,
scarf down salmon like a grizzly,
or blackberries like a bird.
Snuggle close to me at sleep time

telling me stories
about when you were "zero"
and others about Yesterday,
which means the past.

You're proud of learning to read
more words than "ice cream"
and knowing what comes after "forty"
but mostly you want us to read to you.

You bought your cousin a necklace
with your own money.
What a fierce loving human being
you are turning out to be.

Your running toward me
arms ope*n,* when you see me,
yelling *"Nana!"*
made me want to write this poem.

FORTNITE—A HAIBUN

(Fortnite is an online multiplayer video game released in 2017— now with more than 250 million players. Up to 100 players fight to be the last man standing.)

> "A penny arcade
> filled with digitized gunfire
> and children's laughter"
> *—Lester Smith*

Once, lights flickered and a bell rang when you hit the target. Now the targets move faster, through worlds more vivid than the one we live in. You have to kill. If you want, you can pair up with a buddy or two, even if they live in another country. I hear my grandson at his desktop, talking: "Hey, bro, I've got this one."

> Cherry blossom time
> Enthralled children stare at screens
> In their dark rooms

FOUNTAIN OF YOUTH

My old computer
had all its memories——
poems and photos,
conversations with friends——
transferred to a shiny new body
with a brain ten times as quick.

What a metaphor
for its 72-year-old owner!
The idea sustains me—
I will dissolve the boundaries
between us
and feel young again
with infinite possibilities
until we crash.

FOUR SHOOTING STARS ARE ENOUGH

To satisfy our longing–
Brief visitors from outer space
Bringing news of eternity.

FROM QUARANTINE

So where were we
in life's ongoing conversation?
Outside my window,
are the budding trees telling me to stop time,
so I can fully admire them,
or not to stop time,
so they can get on with their growing?
It is hard to remember who needs cheering up,
and to thank the friend who cheered me up.
Things move too fast,
especially when I'm not doing much.
Did I have that debate with you,
or with myself?
My brain is full of thoughts
vying for attention.
Some are good students, some troublemakers.
Stop interrupting!
The more time I spend alone,
the more points of view move in.
I like the company,
find the talk stimulating,
even if sometimes a bit much.
So where were we?

Good-bye

My daughter asked me why
I avoid saying good-bye.
Do I?
Maybe.
I fear the flicker of sadness,
want connection to continue.
There is no need
to emphasize leaving;
just slip away,
and the next thing you know
you are on the street,
buttoning your coat.

And what of the people left—
will they feel abandoned?
I don't like it when someone
disappears from a gathering
without letting *me* know.
Every leaving is a break,
a moment of incompleteness
before I resume being whole again:
Too many loved ones lost
in my childhood,
and I don't want a reminder.

But all these excuses overlook
Good-bye means "God be with ye,"
a blessing I could give and get.

GRANDMA'S PARADOX

One joy of seeing children grow
is watching something important happen
as Time passes by.
On the other hand,
I want Time to
stop.
I love my grandchildren
and am terrified of their adolescence,
when they will disappear.
What can I hold on to
as the subway car of my life
lurches forward?
Forest, age ten, practices narrowing his eyes
with a look that says either
"You don't really expect me to do that,
do you?"
or "That is the most stupid thing I ever heard."
Adorable Shira,
who always liked to play dress-up
and lately to go shopping with Nana,
will soon be adorning herself
to attract the attention of boys
(God help us).
Meanwhile, what will become of me,
caught in Time's jaws, Time's gullet,
Time's small intestine?

Gratitude Is like Blue Salt
(for Norma)

Gratitude is like blue salt
scattered on black ice;
powerful crystals
invade
each frozen slab,
carve them into
crackling slices
I can push away
with my boot,
allowing air to dry
my walkway,
so I can
go on with grace.

HAGAR QIM, MALTA, WINTER SOLSTICE, 2019

I was there when the sun came back,
drew its line, red as embers, on the megalith,
marking winter solstice
on the stone temple wall.
And I wondered how they piled up giant boulders
over five thousand years ago,
without bulldozers?
Who used volcanic glass to cut tabletops?

This year, inside Hagar Qim
as the sun rose and stones began to glow,
I knew I had been here before—
thousands of years before—
watching and cheering,
as happy as I am today
that planting time will come again.

HAIKU

October 2016

No wind—leaves float down
A gust of wind hits the tree
Leaves take flight like thoughts

November 2016

On the ground
bright leaves create beauty
as they die

HOSTING

In my early life, we thought the atom bomb would drop,
so we had to hide under our desks every so often
the way kids nowadays practice for school shootings.
There has always been danger–
sudden pounce of fang and claw–and blood.
Today *I* might be the danger-yes, gentle me-
carrying the invisible virus that will bring *you* down.
How odd to be evil now by being a host,
offering food and warmth.
But my guests feel no obligation to their hostess;
they want to breed and have their babies move on
into someone else.
It's their movie–I am only an extra
In their epic of destruction.

How Can I Know? (Epistemology)

1.
How can I know, stepping out of a cab,
drowsy from a long trip,
that this is really my home?
Trees scribble nonsense with bare branches;
holes appear mysteriously in the blacktop.
I can't turn around; the taxi is gone.

Under a surly moon
that won't light the entry,
the door *seems* recognizable
and the key fits in its lock, but inside,
rooms gasp icy air—
why?

I sit on a suitcase and ponder
how we know *anything*
while someone else fixes the furnace

2.
Five years later, I find it amazing
That half the country thinks
that what the other half thinks are lies.
(I'm in the other half.)
What could I say that would convince anybody
who "knows" that they are right?
I don't know.

So here's a thought: imagine a virus that made people happy instead of killing them. Our virus may give people a little cough, but also tells the brain to make more happy hormones. Happy people hug each other, touch each other, don't stay away. Happy people seek each other out. Another person to infect—good for our virus.

It would be very contagious, unstoppable. Every day, cases doubling, until most of the world was either infected or immune. And happy!

Hurricane Sandy

Warnings abound, with pregnant clouds.

Later, suddenly,
Halloween orgy.
Maples fling limbs ecstatically,
drunk on wind,
branches writhing.

Don't ask me to dance.

Wilder now,
even stately hemlocks bowing.
Gusts come like labor pains,
but nothing is being born.
Tree after tree drops, exhausted.

I stay glued to my window—
suddenly all houses go dark.

I Think Continually

"I think continually of those who were truly great"
—*Steven Spender*

I think continually of those
who lived before me,
having babies under lean-tos, in caves,
who survived saber-toothed tigers
in an ice age.
Now we have central heating,
and our predators are mostly other humans,
whom we can talk to—sometimes—
before they bomb us.

I think continually of those
who lived naked in the jungle.
What kept the insects off?
Now I would be so helpless.
Has the toughness been bred out of us,
or is it still there, under our clothes,
able to preserve our kind
when the time comes
sooner than we would like?

In My Next Life

Do I get to choose?
First: animal or tree?
But will there be a world to rebirth in
with animals, trees, and me?

If not, we could be flames
escaping a supernova
or dark energy between stars
when everything else is over.

Many have seen in the night
millions of twinkling souls
but ignore those who dwell in interstellar gas,
who writhe in a black hole.

Back to the choice I don't have—
part of the cosmic dance.
My next life is tomorrow—
another second chance.

Invasive Species—Haibun

Plants need space to multiply and prosper,
so their colonists traveled the oceans,
found it easy to wipe out the natives:

> Bear claw
> Multiflora rose
> Mile-a-minute vine

skirmish for their place in the sun
as they climb trees, cover them with their own leaves.

> Garlic mustard with battalions of seeds,
> Mugwort deploying underground roots

claim the meadow. We swear and lament
but cannot deny
they are following our example.
The colonists are here to stay.

> Anyone who tells you
> That plants are peaceful creatures
> Lies!

It Is June—Senryo, Haiku

It is June, but I
Have no roses to bring you
Deer found them tasty
Once my buckets overflowed
With many-petaled color

I cannot find the right
Container for my feelings
Perhaps a vase will do

IT'S 1962—A PERSONAL ESSAY

It's 1962 and I want to lose my mind courtesy of LSD, but
I also want to do it right, so I ask Dr. Leary
if I can do "research" and he says, "Sure. Come on up,
stay at our house this weekend."

Charlie Mingus was there too, claimed to have ingested nothing:
"I'm just high on love, Baby."

Linda fed me my sugar cube and also gave one to Ralph,
the philosophy graduate student whose friends had insisted he try LSD
"or you'll never know anything about the nature of reality"

But the minute we swallowed them, before the drug had time to work,
Ralph started screaming, "Stop it!", threw anything he could reach,
and smashed the chandelier.

Tim was afraid the cops would come
so everyone focused on calming Ralph,
ignoring me, while I started to lose my mind,
alone.

Linda finally got Ralph to lie down in her lap
by crooning, "You are a river, I am a river, we are all rivers,"
and the cops didn't come,
but what I learned from my "research"
is that when you take LSD,
do it only with loving friends.

Japanese Death Poem*

For centuries Japanese poets would write a poem just before dying, although some wrote them earlier, to be ready. Warriors carried them into battle. Prince Otsu (663–686) wrote this *tanka* before his execution:

> *This is the last day*
> *I shall see the mallard*
> *Crying over Lake Iware.*
> *Then shall I disappear*
> *Into the clouds**

For the last five hundred years, people have written death poems in haiku form. To prepare myself, and be comforted by these words, I wrote my own:

> Each snowflake drifts down
> Fat as a fingernail
> Then melts on my street

*Note: Translation and citation are from *Japanese Death Poems*, compiled by Yoel Hoffmann, p. 46.

LEONID METEOR SHOWER

I lie down outside
on my towel in the dark, patient.
Stars emerge in their expected places
unless obscured by drifts of cloud.
But tonight I wait for
the rule-breaking flash.
Shake 'em loose!
Bring me chaos!

LIFE STAGES

He does not believe that vitamins
or broccoli make you stronger
He does believe fun is good for you
He is 13 years old

They believe that robots
and computers who know more than we do
will help us live longer and happier
They are 30 years old

When you are 40 you believe
that your children are the greatest
most beautiful and clever
Some are

I wish I believed tomorrow
will be as good as today
or that justice will prevail
I am 70 years old

Manifesto —A Haibun

We all want to be more than our puny selves, to be part of a whole: our clan, a Higher Power. But this search can bring darkness as well as light— every continent except Antarctica has been fertilized with the blood of "unbelievers." Meaning can be found in Nazism as well as the Bible. Nature, of which we are a part, inspires all moods—ecstatic, disgusted. That is why I am a Mysterian, not claiming to be able to make sense of it all, or to claim no sense exists. There are as many meanings as leaves on the trees.

> So many new leaves—
> They block my view of the hills—
> So many colors

MARCH

Sprung from winter's prison—
briefly—
I'm thrown back in the slammer.
Icy wind penetrates my cell.
Why such punishment?
After three months locked up,
I walked in the sun for a week
before an arctic vortex handcuffed me.
When I was let out,
I felt free——fool——

I'm not alone:
Poor innocent buds are caught in the sting.
I beg them: "Please don't open, don't be tricked!
You will turn brown and die."
Some listen, some don't.

But maybe I'm not so innocent.
Perhaps I was petty, selfish, stingy.
Please, let me be deserving
of Spring's longed-for
reprieve.

MARRIAGE

We started out together to explore the Roman Forum,
But now I'm waiting for you to notice I am missing.
Am I an expert in love and marriage
because we have had fifty years together?
A couple I treat are trying to come close to each other
after thirty years and four children.
It's inch by inch.

Issa wrote: *O snail*
              Climb Mount Fuji
              But slowly, slowly
Issa married three times.

Today you called me "Love" (which I like), and I wondered how,
after I screamed at you on Tuesday. Maybe because?

Poems attempt to describe the indescribable—a marriage, for instance.
        Try simile: *Like Penelope's garment—woven, unwoven.*
        Or metaphor: *Diamond, created by pressure.*
        Process: *Conscious hiding, unconscious hiding.*

Can't we keep it simple?
Two people who brush their teeth in the same bathroom?

I'm still waiting for you to *want* to explore the forum *with* me,
Instead of wanting me there to come back to.
        Metaphor: *A balance scale, always tilting.*
                  On one side, together
                  The other, apart
        Simile: *Like our children whose features change as they grow.*
        Process: *Touching, some talking, more touching.*

Memoir
(to Ann Settel)

Speed used to be for boys
racing "shoebox" cars
crashing them into furniture
with uncontrollable laughter

I wanted some of that speed
that freedom
so when I inherited money
I bought me a Porsche,
silver, and named it Shadowfax
(magical horse of Gandalf the wizard)

Shadowfax brought me my husband,
who wanted to drive it on our first date
Oddly enough, I let him
I had said, "No," to all the others.

But thieves drove off with Shadowfax
one night while I was sleeping
I spent the next day wandering the neighborhood,
thinking I was crazy

After that cars became workhorses for me
though not for husband, who enjoyed outrunning the police
flying into a driveway with lights out
while they sped on, pursuing a phantom

Next came the thrill of saving money
driving a car that used teaspoons of gas
and saving the planet at the same time
without even sacrificing speed

Some anxious folk dread driving
never feel the pleasure of losing self in motion
swooping around a corner like a hawk gliding
or leaping like a cheetah when the light changes

MISDEMEANOR

Into how many houses has the moon trespassed
entered through an open window
shaken the stars out of a poet
jumped behind a getaway cloud
and fled

Moonlit Snow

Fingers of new snow
draw fractals on the little tree
outside my back door,
white under the moon,
in a world I don't recognize.

A tourist without even leaving home,
I step outside my door,
camera in hand,
to capture this strange country-
a little frightening in its monochrome tracery,
its looming shadows.
But that's what travel is for:
the shock of the new.
I've seen snowfalls before,
but never *this* postcard,
this light.

New York

The city stays the same; the city always changes.
I was born here, look for remembered landmarks, find them:
Empire State Building,
Central Park—if anything, *more* beautiful—
a row of stores on Lexington Ave,
(but the shopkeepers have changed.)
Still an awesome skyline,
like sacred mountains to the Indians,
Every day, more sun reflecting off glass
blinding, sometimes,
spiritual at sunset.

Some streets are dark and squat the way I expect them to be.
Others I recall as deserted
now flaunt high-rise condos, with doormen.
Riding with tourists recently on top of the double-decker bus,
I saw totally new views from my perch.
Some have been here all my life, but I was never tall enough;
some built yesterday, but I never noticed.
This city is alive
and constantly morphing,
which is why people come here
from towns full of rust or dried-up farms.

I do worship energy-
in people, in the sun, in my hometown.
What was this empty lot once? What will it be?
Nevertheless, I admit I am happy
that I can still look in windows of the building I grew up in,
even if Kitty's toy store is gone.

NEWS HOVERS EVERYWHERE

Someone types, presses *Send,*
and these letters and numbers
pass through my body undetected. . .
tiny bits of information fly into our eyes,
our ears, our nostrils—
faerie dust.
Every breath we take is filled
with symbols we cannot taste.
Like solar wind,
forces out of our control
stay out of sight, out of mind.
We believe we control the broadband—
though we can hardly imagine it.
Perhaps a ribbon, a rainbow?
In Plato's cave, people saw reality
as shadows on the walls;
The first virtual reality!

Now news hovers everywhere,
surrounded by birdcalls.

OCEAN BEACH

(where conscious and unconscious meet—*Anon.*)

Children who play on the beach
don't know they are next to the Mother of All Life,
but nevertheless love to put their feet in the waves
feel the caressing foam.
And sometimes they want to attack waves,
run into them, shouting.
They're lucky if they only get smacked down.
They feel an unconscious pull, like the tides.
Give them a pail and a shovel, and they're happy
to make a castle with a moat around.

So I was upset when my 8-year-old grandson
whined, "No, I don't want to go to the beach."
I thought we had four more years
Before he started rejecting Mommy.

As soon as I learned the word "suburbia," I knew it was a nasty word. A Born in Manhattan elitist, I thought people on the other side of the Hudson River were like cans on a supermarket shelf. In spite of different contents, they were all still cans. They lived in exile because that is where they belonged. I could never live in the suburbs any more than a Royal could become a commoner.

But some Royals get exiled, and that happened when my husband opted to leave the city "for tax reasons." We chose a house with such a perfect view of the city skyline that Jim Henson filmed eight seconds of *The Muppets Take Manhattan* outside our front porch. Only a mile of Hudson River came between me and the city. I did make new friends on my side of the river, but they had the same City center of gravity. We might be in New Jersey, but we were still urban—like Brooklynites now.

After fourteen years, we moved again, now three miles from Manhattan—dangerously far. I couldn't see it any more. But our kids went to high school in the city every day on a school bus, which soothed my fears that I would become one of "them," the "suburbanites." Except I did.

It happened gradually, of course, so I barely noticed. One day when I lamented my favorite supermarket closing, my now college-age daughter sneered: "suburban angst." And she was right, but I didn't care. I had discovered that real people lived here—poets and artists, naturalists and craftsmen, as well as the expected doctors and lawyers—people who were raising families *and* practicing their art.

They weren't famous, but that didn't matter. I wasn't "cutting edge" either, and that didn't matter. What did matter was having friends *and* a garden where I could smell my joyfully tended roses.

ODE TO MY MICROBIOME

I am home to hordes of tiny creatures
who digest what I eat,
give my body what it needs,
keep me alive.

How strange never
to have made their acquaintance.
I don't even know what they look like,
although once I saw little rods
under a microscope.
That was like viewing one person,
and thinking you have seen humanity.

What are their numbers, their language?
How much do they weigh?
Is chocolate good for them?

We are beginning to study this "microbiome"–
their alliances, their wars,
their division of labor.
It's not easy, since they are inside us.
When we die, they die.

Once you know they are there,
life is never the same.
Goodbye, independence;
hello, guilt,
because I had to take antibiotics
for a nasty sinus infection
and proceeded coldly, clear-eyed
to carpet-bomb my gut,
full of innocent friends.

Only Now

All winter frozen
Sleeping
The Life Force
Gets out of bed
And we feel reverberations
Insects appear
From nowhere
Buds swell like pregnant bellies
Purple crocus pops out of the ground

Only now
In this instant
With life rushing in
Death is invisible

Two weeks from now
Death will rise up
Blasting those crocus blossoms

Pebble
(For my father)

"Let me tell you something,"
said the pebble, many-great-grandchild of the mountain.
"Enjoy your days
even when earthquakes loom.
Pick me up and admire me—
I can inspire you to endure—
there is life after a tsunami!
The seas surged for many years to make me smooth and round.
As long as our sun keeps warming the earth,
I'll be tossed around by wind and water
and may end up as sand,
but I will never disappear."

PENT-UP MOTION

Magnolia buds swell inside gray skin
under cold, cloudy skies.
Spring kneels on the starting line
all ready to go, but today's not the day.
Daffodils too are waiting, waiting,
pregnant with unborn yellow.

I feel such impatience—
winter's ropes still bind me.
The birds, those optimists,
fill the air with mating song,
not my howl, "When? When?"
I want us all to explode
in a burst of strength—
sprint into summer.

Personal Ad

I need someone to run with
Someone to make me strive.
I need someone to inspire me
I'm in training to stay alive.

Some people go for the glory
Without which they can't survive.
Not me, I don't have to medal,
I'm in training to stay alive

Distract me when I'm exhausted,
Cheer me when I arrive.
When I want to quit, tell me I'm crazy.
I'm in training to stay alive.

Poet's Paradox

Full moon drinks the wine of night
Fog scowls at me when I try to drive
Stars above shiver not twinkle
Road stretches out
Like linguine

Life brims with metaphors
Seasons come and go each with its simile
Only I
Am unable to be described
By me

PRIVACY

Old houses held sound in their beams
Layers of plaster captured air
Air muffled groans and screams

New apartments tell too much, with scorn
About how many children live upstairs
And what parents did to get them born

As for me, I keep my two lips clenched
Until you've known me a long while
Not exactly secrets, just silence

But young folks now blab all their stuff
To the universe, with pictures too
And the universe can't get enough

Pupa

"A cocoon is a casing spun of silk by many
moths and caterpillars [17] and numerous other ho-
lometabolous insect larvae as a protective covering
for the pupa. Cocoons may be tough or soft, opaque
or translucent, solid or meshlike, of various colors, or
composed of multiple layers, depending on the type
of insect larva producing it. Insects that pupate in a
cocoon must escape from it, and they do this either
by the pupa cutting its way out, or by secreting
enzymes, sometimes called cocoonase, that soften the
cocoon."

—*Wikipedia*

After 12 years, you are ready to come out,
savagely ripping your pupa case.
Mom and Dad have never seen you like this,
while inside, you were quiet and depressed,
stuck inside the white walls, waiting for something
but not sure what. Only reading helped pass the time.
Now, wriggling, you're stuck half in, half out.
It's better than before in spite of being an ordeal
with an unknown end. And it hurts.
I wish I could help, but how?
And anyway, you haven't asked.
Your fierce energy will help you escape
into spring sunshine
where love is waiting for you.

Rafi

He uses his superpowers to zap his sister;
I once used mine to save the world
but the world refused to be saved.

Only four years old, he makes you
want to hold and protect him,
but all *he* wants to do is fight bad guys
and *anything* can be a bad guy—

a block, a toy car, even a pebble
is there to be overcome by Superman
(he's not particularly into fighting people),
and I look at Rafi my love and think

war will always be with us.
On any continent, half of all babies being born
Have this Y chromosome that wants to fight
And *win*. Evolution rewards winners

with women (and babies) and
land and gold to feed them. Women are programmed
to love the fighters too,
reward them with kisses and more babies

And then the babies grow
first into superheroes,
then muscle up into real heroes,
killing real people, incidentally releasing
real blood, real grief.

REGRETS

Once, on the Appalachian Trail
I stepped on an orchid,
and when I was sixteen
I failed to stop a bully.

I was never extravagant,
even when I could afford it;
never had a Black or Asian lover.

I wonder
if I was to blame (the way my kids say I was)
for their teenage angst.
Perhaps I could have done more to help.

And I *really* wonder,
What am I doing or not doing
right now
that I will one day regret?

REPEATING MY DREAM

"My dream repeats itself."
—*Jorie Graham*

I dreamed I could wake up virtually,
let my heavy body turn over
and go back to sleep
while my image throws its feet
over the side of the bed, stands up,
drags downstairs to make oatmeal.

My dream repeats itself.
I wish it would tell me
what kind of day I was going to have:
all chores, or old friends calling?
Sunshine or gray? In other words,
worth waking up for?

In coronavirus lockdown
nothing much happens
to make my body want to move-
let my image do the laundry.

Perhaps I could keep repeating my dream
until the world recovers
from *its* bad dream.

RULES—A HAIBUN

"Who makes the rules around here?"
asks my 12-year-old granddaughter.
"There shouldn't be any.
I would make a world without rules."
I try to make her think:
"Don't we need traffic lights?
Stop on the red, go on the green."
Then I recall, in New York City,
car stop on red, but people don't.
Or Naples, where cars run the light,
and people take their chances.
"What about the Golden Rule?" I say,
then decide it's more of a suggestion than a rule,
given how it's followed.
I know she is tired of being bossed around,
but if she got what she wanted,
what would she do—
boss *me* around?
I have an idea:
What about the Ten Commandments?"
She points out, *"Moses broke the tablets."*
It's hard to design a world
with freedom to do what you like
that everybody likes.

March. Robins return.
If only good behavior
Was so dependable.

Run-On Sentence

Life isn't lived in sentences,
but we stuff what happens into them,
cram an ocean into a pond,
a tree into a leaf,
not something you would do even if you could,
because the world needs oceans and trees
as well as words;
and music, too, is a way of describing
what happened today to Jimmy and me,
although I bet Jimmy would write a song about it,
because he says a song makes you feel a thought;
and if I think of painters
who tried to capture the events of a whole day
in a single frame—
Brueghel maybe—even he must have left something out,
but not being a painter,
I can't figure out how one could draw time,
although artists did make "happenings"
though time sneaks off stage
at every opportunity,
so perhaps it really is best to use words like
"First this happened,
and then that happened,"
although it is hard to know
how much to say,
or when to stop,
so I recommend just living your life
without worrying too much
about telling your story
or how it is going to end.

SEEDLINGS—A HAIBUN

A pair of cute lime-green "seed leaves" open, giving no clue, like toddlers, how tall the grown-up will be, or how pretty, or how useful. But the little leaves poke through brown dirt, announcing, "I'm here."

> Tiny foxglove sprout
> Creates its own baby food
> From air, water, sun

SEEKING MAGIC

My three-year-old audience
evokes stories
from a place in my brain
well hidden,
carpeted with moss.

These stories have magic:
Magic boots, magic lollipops,
even a magic escalator.

No magic in *my* dreams lately:
I dreamed I was taking out the trash.
But when I look into Maia's wide eyes,
I know how to make her fly.

Chapter Three was too scary.
"Every good story," I tell her,
"has to be scary in the middle
but happy at the end."
I just hope I don't die in the middle.

Her story now is on Chapter Nine.
We have overcome fearsome obstacles.
What do *I* want?
Mysterious portal
to unlimited worlds. . .

And what do you think happened next?

SELF-PORTRAIT IN FOUR DIMENSIONS

Some days I am round and juicy
Some days made of parchment paper
Some days a fine line drawing
Some days, simply pointless.

SEPARATION

"Separation, you set fire in the heart and home of every lover."

—anonymous Afghan poet

I. *Travel Journal*

An infant, leaving Mama, howls.
Later, we travel
in order to separate from home.

Most people, like turtles,
take their home with them
just to be safe. They are called "tourists."

I travel searching for new experience
but everyone on the plane
looks like someone I know.

It isn't that I want to be safe—
it's that everyone I left
needs me to keep them safe.

Nonsense!
Fasten the seat belt
for your inner child.

. .

Longing for home
was a fire in the heart
but not now, on this beach,

as a Polynesian man
flaunts his beautiful blue tattoo
on a dark chest.

2. *Ashes in the Heart*

You went to Chiapas the summer of our junior year
to dig up, what–bones? Pots?
Doing what you loved,
leaving me in New York, my home,
contemplating medical school,
filling up time with an empty volunteer job
calling surgeons out of the OR
when all I could see over their masks
was eyebrows,
so of course I didn't know who was who,
and got fired.

You were learning the ways of the Mayans,
which is what you wanted,
while I waited for the mail–
delicious long letters at first,
then shorter,
then a postcard:
"What can I say?"

I had to act normal
because I was living at home,
mother hovering, anxious.
I had to wake up every day, get out of bed,
walk out the door;
I couldn't tell her the house was burning.

SHALOM BAYIT

I work long hours with this warring couple—
to help him see how much she cares,
to help her see how hard he tries.
Unfortunately, throwing arrows makes him come alive;
and throwing them back makes her feel safe.
Good people, of course, who just want to be happy
but, like the English and the Irish,
nurse anger over past injustice.

His father taught him Life is War
so that is how he lives,
seeing silent battles even in the suburban sunset
or in his wife's choice of fish for dinner.
As a child she was never allowed to talk back,
so now she enjoys spitting bullets,
practicing her idea of adulthood.

But they both say their goal is *shalom bayit,*
which means "peace in the home."
So we soldier on
turning swords into serving spoons.

Sheltering in Place

The usual fiery globe of setting sun,
turns clouds into their evening purple—
but as I sit and open my window
to toss out a misplaced ant without killing it,
a pink glow circles my window frame
in a way I have never seen.
I notice more, staying home.

An almost ordinary sunset in extraordinary times.
What did I expect? Heat and smoke?
The demon killing people is invisible.
Now sun is a half melon sinking into the hills.
I can say, "See you tomorrow, sun," as usual,
but tonight add, "I hope."

SILENCES

Forest before a storm—silence
Meadow after a snowfall—silence
The silence in between breaths

Silence of a couple
Asleep after making love
Silence of gratitude or awe

Meditation hall.
In silence seekers connect
with what some call God

SNOW

Look! The white sky dumped white
up to your thighs.
Sparrow tracks engrave hieroglyphics

Atmospheric physics can predict it
but only language
changes snow into tablecloths and bedsheets,
moonscapes and deserts,
while our eyes watch it
bury or transform.

While you shovel,
let these thoughts divert you
from winter's icy
reality.

SOLSTICE ANNIVERSARY

It's our anniversary tomorrow
and winter solstice the next day.
I always write a solstice poem
but I've never written an anniversary poem
to *you*.

Why not? I wonder. I've had 42 chances,
all passed up.
We both agreed to ignore anniversaries,
and did.

We worried about being "married"
Would we become stodgy and boring
like our parents? Become a "husband" and "wife,"
not ourselves?

Let it be out of sight, out of mind:
the fact that we did sign the contract
because I wanted kids, and didn't mind
the idea of some red tape
binding us.

So why today? What's changed?
Could it be your recent brush with death
in and out of hospital,
fear of being cut down never far from
our minds?

Or could it be the solstice-
blue-gray sunset tonight-
when the sun stands still briefly,
then begins again its ascent into
a new year?

Each moment is always new,
but this year everything will be more new
because you have never been sick
with anything before. This calls for a
new poem—

one about forty-three years
of being together—
whatever you want to call it—
even "anniversary." Let's celebrate.
We made it!

SOMEDAY YOU'LL REMEMBER THIS

Someday you'll remember this,
my mother said, trying to shame me,
and I thought, *I hope so*—
but now I'm not so sure.
Memories
are like knots that have to be tied,
and someone has been untying mine—
only a few stars in an otherwise dark sky,
like the four hours we spent in a sex motel
while a babysitter stayed with the kids.

I do remember, years ago, Mom telling me
that if I didn't learn to make my bed
no one would want to marry me.
That didn't make sense even at the time.
But the worst curse was:
"Someday your children will treat you
the way you treat me."
It happened, of course, but only for a day—
enough, I hoped, to fulfill the curse.

Yesterday you asked, "Do you remember, when we met,
standing on the street corner on 79th Street,
gazing into each other's eyes?"
And actually, I do.

Sonnet: Spring Lament 2014

If the sun shines only approximately
Of what shall I speak? What cheerful tunes
Warble to you? And then what gravity
Holds us together ? Our frozen moon
Shines now and then. How can I ever know
What's coming next? Today a little bird
Sang in the morning, even though more snow
Is expected. Carry on, through the absurd
Gray chill. What kind of lyric can I sing,
When all I want is to crawl into bed
Covered with down blankets? This is spring?
Lying there, I thought I might be dead,
But I am not, I'm dormant. I withstood
Long shadows. Now, sun, shine the way you should!

Spring 2014

It happened again—
I spent weeks
fretting she wouldn't come,
would break the engagement,
change her mind.
And then
Spring ran away with me

SPRING WON'T STAY

"Grief. . .you whose task it is to let nothing be lost."
—*Jim Glaser*

Spring won't stay,
won't keep tuning up its green symphony,
weaving light between buds.
On the first hot day, those cherry blossoms–
imagined for so many barren months–
will drop.

Spring is extravagant,
spending its triumphal emergence
without fear of bankruptcy
scattering petals like silver dollars
pollen like pearls.

Spring won't stick around in slow-mo
as the sun pulls up life.
Spring will spiral into another season
also lovely, of course, but not shocking,
not thick with gratitude for release.

Joy has no care for the future
when the present is exquisite.
Only grief lets nothing be lost.

STARTING TO LOOK AT MY EARLY JUNE GARDEN—A HAIBUN

> "The ten thousand things" is a Chinese expression used to
> mean the indefinite multitude of all forms and beings in manifest
> existence. Thus, it denotes the fecundity of the all-creative maya,
> boundless abundance of Our Mother God."
> —*www.mother-god.com/ten thousand things*

Here I see empty spaces,
so full of possibility for color or chaos.
There, ghosts of past glories, eaten by deer.
Deer won't go near my basil, chives, or mint
-strong scent masks danger.
Bell-shaped foxgloves, so beautiful, so poisonous.
Morning glory tendrils wave in the air, looking for support.
Little seedlings—plant or weed?
I'll let both stay for now—both cute.
Grape vines, Virginia creeper—get out, before I pull you out!
Extravagant pink peonies, tiny terrestrial orchids.
Imagine plucking cherry tomatoes
where now you see white blossoms.
Behind all, spiky leaves of daffodils—
Flowers gone, like April and May.

> Sunlit day in June
> The Ten Thousand Things—right here
> In my own garden

STINGY OLD SUN—HAIKU

Stingy old sun
In a February sky—
Give alms! Give alms!

STUFF

I can't get rid of stuff
It embodies me
Two attics and two basements are filled with
my former selves:
books I loved
papers I wrote
thousands of photographs
There's also the little wine bottle Diana brought me
(covered with dust)
and notes I no longer understand
explaining higher mathematics
clothes I wore when I wanted to impress people
who wanted to impress me
and whom I no longer know

I don't believe those days will come again
but without these physical presences
perhaps none of that happened

I want to live in the present
I don't want to live in the past
But I don't want the past to disappear
the way it will when I toss out my stuff

My aging friends are all getting rid of stuff
so their children won't have to do it when they're gone
I would rather have my kids do it
because when I'm gone, I won't care
and everything they recycle will be just stuff

Suddenly Deaf

Fluid fills spaces where air should be
eardrums can't tremble.
I live in a murmuring universe
absorbed in thought
as I pass through odds and ends of sound.

The people at the next table
could be monkeys or parrots
chattering in this jungle restaurant.
Near and dear continue to mumble
until I realize it's OK
they are talking to themselves.

Amazing how little is said that is important
not like sunlight on wet grass
or the touch of your hand.

Summer Solstice Fragments

1.
One cloud a velociraptor
One a kangaroo
Chases the sun where it set
Behind the hill
Catches it
Light lingers
Impossibly

2.
Enlightenment means light all day

3.
Night
Has been whittled away
And the moon climbed to the strangest place
Flavored with honeysuckle and rose
Treetops like clouds in the moonlight
And the birds sang at 5:00 a.m.
When the sky turned pink

If death is eternal darkness
This is the antideath

Summer Solstice Vigil

> "Sun at the solstice halts in its tracks—
> Midsummer twilight lingers like a dream..."

7:05 p.m.—The sun plays blinding tag in and out of leaves
7:30—The sky, washed-out blue like an old sheet
      Sun keeps twinkling
7:35—Breezes begin their music. Solar wind?
      Though behind glass, I think I hear it and my skin tingles
7:45—At the tip of the sky I see little pink—or is it orange?
7:55—High oak branches begin to glow

Stay entranced
so the light may never end

8:20—I can stare at the orange sun
      as it slips behind my neighbor's house
8:25—Outside, I still cast a faint shadow

8:31-*Official sunset*

No fanfare, only green silhouettes of trees,
A little ominous against the bright sky
My 15 hours of daylight are over
But "civil twilight" allows gardening, encourages strolling
In the East, one white cloud pretends it is still day
Though indoors, lights go on
A tricky time

8:41—First fireflies
      On the lawn, among the roses
8:42—Everybody's automatic lights turned on
      but the streetlights did not
      From inside, dark shadows make it look

as if you need a lantern to walk
But you don't

9:00 p.m.—No streetlight yet, but fireflies brilliant
        Against dark ivy
9:05—Dark outside my window, but high up to the west,
        orange
9:20—I see the streetlight come out, like a star
9:25—Still a glow in the west
9:30—*Dark, finally*

Start the Fireworks!

Swimming In Long Island Sound—
Five Days In July

1.

How could I not be blessed
when a river of gold follows me?

                                How could I not be happy?
                                No jellyfish, high tide

Sky, water, children
All beautiful

2.

Moving with the current I am strong-
Taoist swimming

                                Opening my eyes underwater
                                I see creation

Here there are no politics
Only life and death

3.

I float on my back in the sky–
Sunset swim

                  Drifting with the current
                  gliding through spacetime

between the slightly nibbled moon
and the smeared sun

4.

The plane goes one way
Clouds and I the other

                  I swim toward my shining future
                  which appears and disappears

Calm gray-green water
Unseen current against me

5.

Far from shore
A monarch butterfly
Checks me out

Steely gray day
and this is still exactly
where I want to be

Swimming with six swans
I want what I have –
July swimming

TEEN-AGE READER—A HAIBUN

Young adult books need
an appealing hero, confused at first,
or stymied, or worse. The novels must have
a little sex and, of course,
something about love.

By the end our hero has escaped the trap,
jumped the obstacles,
learned not to be afraid of sex,
and-we hope-
not to be afraid of love—
unless there is a sequel.

Hypnotized by her novel,
she does not look up.
What is she learning?

THE COST OF LIVING

We don't buy "living."
After we're born,
it happens.

We don't know the price—
of our food (soil exhausted)
or our shelter (oaks cut down)
of every something new we must have

Life is a gift-
unbearably expensive,
gratefully accepted.

Goodbye Again to the Golden Boy—A Haibun
(Donald Morris Bahr, 1940–2016)

I loved you dearly. Why don't I care very much that you died? Could be that it's 55 years since I last saw you, but that's not it. More to the point: time long ago devoured the boy I loved.

I still see you striding tall down the beach– blond, gorgeous in your black wool cape– or painting my abstract portrait (fully clothed, no face.) What a wonderful/terrible year of joy and torture we had, although your leaving me was entirely awful.

Fifteen years later, you wrote you were coming to my city, did I want to see you? A hard question–you were still dangerous, for better and worse. I had a husband, and two kids, so I wrote:

"I love you and hate you and don't want to see you."

At our college 50th reunion I prayed you would not come. In fact, you were at home, very ill. I dreaded meeting an old man; I wanted to remember that perfect boy.

> We met on a June beach
> Waves still roll in without us
> Cold sand underfoot

THE PRICE OF CLEAR VISION

"How clearly do you want to see?"
asked the optometrist.
"I want to see it all," I said,
so he fitted my glasses
and turned me loose on the world.

Outside his office I see
cigarette butts
stuck between slabs of pavement,
yellow and white plastic bags
everywhere.

Driving home,
I can't keep my eye on the road.
Every penthouse tells a story.
A peregrine falcon
perches next to the highway.

Home, finally, free to stop focusing,
I see the future war in Asia,
mushroom cloud rising.

I return to the optometrist.
"Not quite so clear," I say.

The Road Not Taken—A Haibun

Zihuatenejo was a deserted beach paradise in Mexico, and I had been invited to go there. Azure water, curve of white sand and palm trees, birds—you can see it, no? Who wouldn't want to go, especially if one had a summer between semesters with no plans. There was one problem—my parents were dead-set against it.

I tried to convince them that I would be all right: "They are professors at Harvard. They know what they are doing." Unfortunately my parents also knew what the professors were doing: studying LSD. "You'll be taking drugs." "It's ground-breaking research, Mom. They will be famous! And I have a chance to be in at the beginning."

I couldn't let Mom know I also had some doubts about the project, namely, that my brain could get fried. Timothy Leary and Richard Alpert *were* professors, but they were also a little kooky, risk-takers. Still, I felt excited and flattered that'd they asked me to go with them. I didn't exactly need my parents' permission, but I didn't want to defy them either. I wasn't 100% a rebel; 50% maybe. So I dragged out making my decision.

While I was stalling, Leary and Alpert got kicked out of Mexico —something about a murder. Just think: I might have been there—but I'm sure the charges were trumped up.

Now Zihuatenejo is a popular tourist destination, and I am the doctor I wanted to become. That deserted beach is lined with hotels I never want to see.

> This stream has two branches
> One will dry up in summer
> I must guess—which?

THE UNSEEN ELEMENTS

> "What is essential is invisible to the eye."
> —Antoine de Saint-Exupéry, *The Little Prince*

Fire:

look into the burning woodstove—
you can't show me where blue-edged orange flames
become heat.

Air:

only indirectly visible
when we see it push billowing sails,
bend oaks in a hurricane.

Earth and Water:

we think we know
but scientists say
when you look closely
at the space inside their atoms,
invisible forces
hold everything together.

So celebrate the known world.
Let us cling to each other
as if we were solid
even if we are being fooled.

To Walter With Gratitude

I hadn't seen you or heard your voice
for 53 years.
This week in a report of our high school 60th reunion,
I saw you, with your wife.
You're alive!
When I recently tried looking for you on the internet
the last reference was 20 years old,
which had really worried me.

Now, I wonder, why do I care so much?
What do I get from feeling your presence in the world?

If you are alive,
part of me is still alive—
consciousness emerging from childhood,
beautiful as a tulip,
passionate about ideas, scared of sexual feelings;
I barely remember her. You knew her well.
If you die, she dies.

We shepherded each other through some dangerous valleys—
tough teenage years—
oblivious to the peril
while so many were scarred.

You tried to teach me chess;
we listened to Schubert's *Trout Quintet*.
What did I teach *you*?
That you were loveable,
and that is what you taught *me*--
more reason to be glad
you are still here.

TRAFFIC

Sitting in a tin box, unable to move
when I should be speeding
along the highway of life or 32nd Street.
Imprisoned behind a garbage truck
when I should be free-wheeling
down the avenue of life, or Broadway.

"Beware the word *should*,"
I tell my patients
who use it to multiply their suffering,
by thinking that their husband—or life—
isn't treating them the way he-or-it
"should."

So I could, while stuck on the road,
see how rosy light beams off windows,
listen to soothing music-
even write a poem
and not mind the honking behind me
when I fail to leap ahead on the green.

Trail Guide

On the wooded path, I ask my group
where food comes from.
"The supermarket," says a wise-ass
to cover up the fact he doesn't know.

I tell them
nothing can live without the sun.
We look up
through the tree canopy
at the sun playing hide-and-seek.
They are unimpressed.
They are 8 years old,
All they care about are animals.

I try again:
You drink milk (from cows)
and eat hamburgers (from steer)
but cows and steer must eat grass
and grass needs sun to grow.

Blank eyes.

They have never known a world without sun,
never hidden under a trap door like Anne Frank
or crouched in a solitary cell.
I would not wish it on them,
But I want them to know the truth.

We emerge from the forest
into a sunny meadow
humming with dragonflies,
bees on the clover.
They take off their sweaters—
begin to get it.

Two Realities

I'd rather slip out of a dream than into it.
My dreams run endless loops, like Mobius strips
that only end when I get up for a snack.

Teenagers wait for "real life" to start,
but I'm on that fast track and want to sit down
by the window, watching real life of birds.

Ugly Poem

My mind yesterday
Nursing home inmates
Bombed-out buildings
Post-tornado houses

My mind this morning
Rusty machinery
Misshapen children
Three-day-old roadkill

Abandoned cities. . .
Where is the end to this?
Surrounded by beauty
In tonight's setting sun

Usually Spring

Usually Spring
Bursts on the winter landscape
Like a diva on stage

Usually Spring
Comes to my birthday party
Holding armloads of cherry blossoms

Usually Spring
Speeding along
Knocks me off my bicycle

But this year
Spring hides in a corner
Refusing to budge

Forsythia
Always gold by now
Keeps its buds closed

I wanted to slow
Time's rushing stream,
But I never wanted it to dry up

WAITING

I'm good at waiting.
So many people get angry or bored.
I could teach them
how to look through eyeholes
as through a train window,
how to be a tourist
and notice, notice, notice;
how to feel breath enter
and leave the body–
waves that can be surfed, slowly–
or how to leave this place entirely,
travel in time or space.

No wonder my family chooses me
to stand on line at Disney World
while everyone else goes shopping.
I have useful skills
they could be practicing
while we wait.

WALKER IN LATE WINTER

Claws of ice grab at my toes.
This winter's snow is in slow retreat,
possibly planning to regroup and attack again.
I scan with eagle eye for signs of new life,
but my eagle would starve if dinner depended on it.
The ivy, supposedly evergreen, turned brown.
It is very hard now to believe in Spring
but easier than believing in God,
because my own eyes have seen it,
even if that was long ago.

WHEN DOES IT STOP?—A HAIBUN

All the music I never heard is out there in the internet cloud, and in the minds of millenials I never met——more music, more strangers every day, squeezing me into irrelevance.

So many books I'll never know are published every week. I like to read about some of them, see them mentioned in reviews before they retreat into the cloud, countless.

It was not always so: In ancestral tribes we lived in groups of 50 to 200, mostly interrelated. All the stories were memorized, songs and dances repeated at harvest time. Everyone was important: best runner, funniest, meanest. . . .

There simply hasn't been enough time, enough eons of evolution, for my brain to cope with personal insignificance.

> Dark summer sky:
> I keep counting the stars
> As fast as I can

WHEN THE MESSIAH COMES—A HAIBUN

When the Messiah comes, I say, "What took you so long?
People are suffering. Get to work, fast, now!"
But He doesn't move. What is He waiting for?
He looks around, as if to say,
"Is this the world I'm supposed to save?"
And I hope He won't be overwhelmed
by our intransigence, our stupidity.

> When spring arrives
> Grass pushes through concrete slabs
> Hope becomes visible

WHERE DO NIGHTMARES GO?—A HAIBUN

Where do nightmares go?
I wonder as I sit up.

Do I really want to know?
The scene that seemed so real
seconds ago has vanished.
This bed feels solid.
I am afraid to go back to sleep.
"Thank God it was only a dream."

But what if, in another universe,
I'm living it and don't wake up?
This happens to many people.
I saw them on the news last night,
staring at cinders that were their home;
or others, swept away in a flood,
thinking, Wake up, wake up.

      winter fog
      you disappeared
      just after we said goodnight

Winter Solstice Sunrise

"Solstice" is derived from the Latin phrase for "sun stands still."
That's because—after months of growing shorter and lower—the
sun's arc through the sky appears to stabilize. Then the arc begins
growing longer and higher.

6:35 a.m.—There they are—rosy fingers of cloud, black sky becoming
       blue as a dream.
6:40 a.m.—Azure now, the sky says I am not dreaming, the sun will
       come.
Trees sketch their designs against a luminous backdrop
while the great lighting designer in the sky tugs at our emotions:
Praise be!

6:50 a.m.—Outside the window, the spruce begins to turn green,
       and so does the birdfeeder's metal roof.
No birds, though. They will wait.
Now the clouds are gray against a watery blue background;
a few leaves still on the copper beech hang brown.
Even on the west side of the house,
the neighbor's car has turned red, as have the barberries.

In only 15 minutes, the world has been transformed
partly by sun's return, partly by knowledge
of what this means today.
I'm no shepherd—just woke up early—
but there's no doubt about the miracle to happen.
Planes leaving La Guardia, flashing their lights
will have to substitute for heavenly hosts,
their roar for Hosannas.

7:17 a.m.—Look! Shadows!

WINTER SUNSET THOUGHTS

Early afternoon
I see our sun drop
red behind the pines

Winter solstice
Sun shines colors into sky
before going away

And I ask myself
Can I go down
so beautifully

WOUND

It's open and stays open, red meat.
Every day I change the bandage, peer in:
Maybe a little smaller today?
Circle of skin growing tighter?
Odd to be so incomplete, so imperfect.
All those years I walked around perfect,
Never knew it.
The hole grief makes is like this:
Hurting like Hell at first, crippling,
then able to be ignored at times,
closing imperceptibly.
Will either heal completely?
If I had to place my bet,
it would be on the visible wound
in my flesh.

First Job—A Haibun

I am pasting whiskey bottle labels
on government forms
over and over again
and the boss comes by
gloating: "So this is what
you went to college for?"
I don't reply.

Really, I did learn a lot from that job
when I went to the Christmas party,
where Dave, quite drunk
confided that he was trapped in this job
because the boss depended on him,
would never promote him,
threatened to blackball him
if he ever tried to leave.

That is when I decided to go to medical school.

> The salmon leaps upstream
> To the place where it can spawn
> Some don't make it

Confessions of an Easygoing Soul

Show me a short cut, and I will take it;
Don't wrestle with the Devil
if you can blow his brains out first.
I'm no hero; he who hesitates
may live to try another day.
If you give me an inch,
I'll be happy with it;
if you lead me to water and want me to drink,
make sure it's delicious.
I will definitely look before I leap,
but then again, I may not leap at all,
if I like it here.

THE POET'S LAMENT—A HAIBUN

Help me! Every living thing begs to be described.

> If only I could
> Grasp what the stream is saying—
> It won't speak clearly!

Can I loosen the grip of grammar, break out of logic's box? Dreams produce great poems – that disappear. Schizophrenics' "word salad" can be beautiful– but crazy. A poem without words would be "music" –another frequency altogether.

> My hearing is poor
> The stream recites a poem—
> I miss every word.

THEMES

Someone said all poems are about Time,
which is true if you want to stretch it.
Seasons (I particularly like the solstices,
and spring and the rest), definitely.
Flowers: sure-Old Masters would put a symbolic
wilting flower in their paintings.
Children: you bet.
Aging: do you have to ask?
People: well, they age and die. Animals, too.
Self: same.
Things people do, or think about: moments in time.
Coronavirus: same (at least we hope it won't last forever).
So, you see, that sage someone knew all my themes,
But my poem about the internet—
no Time there that *I* can see
sneaked past him or her.

ABOUT THE AUTHOR

Annette Hollander, M.D., is a psychiatrist who lives in Englewood, New Jersey. Her first book, *How to Help Your Child Have a Spiritual Life,* was published in 1980 by A&W Press and was a selection of the Young Parents' Book Club. The urge to write resurfaced after she and her husband raised two daughters who began building their own nests. By 2010 she had enough poems to publish her first book, *Scenes From My Trip: Poems 1998-2010.*

As Coronavirus became a pandemic in 2020, she decided it was time for another book with the next ten years of poems, so she wouldn't die before she could do a final edit.